Kalungi Ssebar.

ASSATA TAUGHT ME

a fictional play inspired by the FBI's Most Wanted Woman

OBERON BOOKS
LONDON

WWW.OBERONBOOKS.COM

First published in 2017 by Oberon Books Ltd
521 Caledonian Road, London N7 9RH
Tel: +44 (0) 20 7607 3637 / Fax: +44 (0) 20 7607 3629
e-mail: info@oberonbooks.com
www.oberonbooks.com

A catalogue record for this book is available from the British Library.

PB ISBN: 9781786821096
E ISBN: 9781786821102

Dedicated to my Jajja (Grandma)
Lucy Namatovu, may you continue to rest in power.

Would like to thank my family, especially my mum for being so unconditionally supportive and my brother Moses Ssebandeke for giving me that extra push I needed to write this play. A special thanks to Talawa for opening their doors to me. I must also say a massive thank you to The Gate team, with Christopher Haydon at the helm for making their resources available. One final BIG thank you to Lynette Linton for her infectious enthusiasm towards my writing and of course Assata Shakur whose story sparked the flame that got the fire burning.

Characters

ASSATA SHAKUR
Sixties: Black Revolutionary in exile

FANUCO MACEO
Twenty-one: Young disillusioned black Cuban, her student

ACT ONE

Over blackout we hear a 1980's documentary on ASSATA SHAKUR. It details briefly her life pre-Black Panther Party, the fatal shooting on the New Jersey Turnpike, the prison sentence & escape and catches us up on her current situation living in political exile in Cuba.

SCENE 1

March 14th 2016

Very late in the night.

Lights go up on ASSATA who stands cleaning the wounds of a bloodied FANUCO who sits almost unperturbed by the whole situation.

Pause.

FANUCO: You should see the other guy.

ASSATA: I saw them. They didn't have a scratch.

FANUCO: It wasn't a fair fight.

ASSATA: That was a *fight*? Looked more like an initiation.

FANUCO: ?

ASSATA: You don't know what that is do, you?

FANUCO: No.

ASSATA: You're right. Three on one isn't fair.

FANUCO: They're lucky you stepped in. I was just about to…

> *He does a right jabbing motion. It brings him more pain in his ribs.*

ASSATA: Sit still before you break yourself.

FANUCO: They don't know that Fanuco Maceo is the young Cuban Muhammad Ali.

> *(In his best Muhammed Ali impression.)*

I am the –

ASSATA: If you could be the quietest, that would be great.

FANUCO: Sorry.

ASSATA: Unless you want them to come back for round two.

FANUCO: No. No, I don't.

ASSATA: Fanuco Maceo?

FANUCO: Si. Like Antonio Maceo.

> *Silence.*

The Bronze Titan? He fought in –

ASSATA: Yes, I know him.

FANUCO: Okay.

> *Silence.*

He was my great grandfather.

> *Silence.*

My uncle has his name.

> *Silence.*

Thank you, madam…?

ASSATA: Assata.

FANUCO: You sound like you are American.

ASSATA: Yup.

FANUCO: I love America.

> *Silence.*

My uncle Antonio lives in Miami and he says it's amazing. Especially the wo – weather.

ASSATA: Cuba has amazing…weather too.

FANUCO: Forgive me, madam.

ASSATA: What for?

FANUCO: For talking about the…weather in front of you.

ASSATA: Hey, talk about the weather all you want. Just as long as you give it the respect it deserves.

FANUCO: Yes, madam.

> *Silence.*

I must have a face that people like to hate.

ASSATA: Hate or Hit?

> *Thinks about it for a very short while.*

FANUCO: Same thing.

Thank you for standing up for me.

ASSATA: That's fine. I'm sure you would have done the same for me.

FANUCO: I'm not sure I would find the right words to stop three guys from hitting you.

ASSATA: You never know what you can or can't do until you're face to face with fate.

FANUCO: So you think it's fate that we met?

> *She doesn't answer.*

How come you was in Old Havana at that time in the night?

ASSATA: Where else would I be?

FANUCO: Here. Where it's safe.

> *She finishes tending to his wounds. Doesn't even bother answering his initial question.*

ASSATA: How are you feeling?

FANUCO: Great. So wha –

ASSATA: Good. So you can go home now.

FANUCO: Oh. Okay. Well, encantado, madam Assata.

ASSATA: Nice to meet you too, Fanuco Maceo.

FANUCO: Oh you don't have to call me that. Just call me Blackie.

>   *Beat.*

ASSATA: You let people call you that?

FANUCO: Yes, because I am –

ASSATA: Yes I get it.

Well you better be going…Fanuco.

>   *He goes to correct her but decides not to before exiting.*
>
>   *ASSATA goes to double lock her door.*
>
>   *She then approaches the picture of her grandmother that sits carefully on her cabinet. She delicately picks it up and begins speaking to it.*

Harsh? I saved the boy from a beating what else did he want? A lolly pop? He will find his way back okay. This is Havana not Wilmington. I'm sure he will be home in no time. It's late, Grandma. I'm gonna go to sleep. Good night.

>   *She kisses the photo before placing it back to its original place.*
>
>   *She then makes towards her bedroom, turning off the lights before she exits.*

SCENE 2

March 15th 2016

Morning.

ASSATA sits in her rocking chair reading a poetry book.

Music from her music player plays in the background.

Suddenly it's interrupted; we hear (in Spanish) discussions about Obama's imminent visit to Cuba next week.

She reacts to it.

A knock on her door startles her.

It persists, almost impatiently.

She slowly puts down her poetry book, turns the radio off, walks towards the window where she keeps her gun and makes to draw for it.

ASSATA: Who is it?

FANUCO: *(Offstage.)* It's me, bl – Fanuco. Fanuco Maceo? We met last night.

        She unlocks the door.

ASSATA: Boy, I remember you.

    What are you doing here?

        He takes out his school book.

FANUCO: My professor set me an assignment.

    She asked me and only me to write a paper on why moving to the US is better than staying in Cuba.

        Pause.

ASSATA: Why are you telling me this?

FANUCO: Oh. Yes. See, after you kicked me out –

ASSATA: Sent you home.

FANUCO: After you sent me home, I had an idea. You are American. Maybe you can tell me all the good things about America and I put them in my essay.

ASSATA: The good things about America?

FANUCO: Yes.

ASSATA: Fan –

FANUCO: Let me read you the essay first before you say no.

He takes in a deep breath then begins to read.

My name is Fanuco Maceo, I am twenty-one years old. I am from Central Havana where I live with my mother and father and little sister, Celia who will be turning twelve this year.

My father is currently falling sick and my mother has to stay home to take care of him.

I am in my last year of the Criminal Law course at the University of Havana. And I'm excited because with this degree I can go and find work in Miami where I have an uncle who will be hiring me.

She shuts the door in his face.

FANUCO: *(Offstage.)* So, what did you think?

She's slightly enamoured by his persistence but won't let on.

She decides to open the door to him.

ASSATA: Fanuco, what do you want?

He decides to come clean.

FANUCO: I want you to be my teacher.

Short pause.

ASSATA: Teacher? Teacher of what?

FANUCO: English and everything to do with America.

ASSATA: You're English sounds pretty good to me.

FANUCO: But I don't want it to sound good. I want it to sound GREAT! You speak so beautiful. Like a poet.

She lets him in.

ASSATA: Where did you get the idea that I was a teacher?

FANUCO: I got it just when I was walking by –

ASSATA: No. I mean why do you think I am a teacher?

FANUCO: You are American. Or else why are you living in Cuba if you are not teaching?

ASSATA: I could be a journalist.

FANUCO: Hahaha. You are not a journalist. How can you be? You are not white.

Silence.

So… you will teach me?

ASSATA: No.

He's visibly upset.

Well no point getting all upset about it.

FANUCO: Why not? You think my English is so bad that I am unteacheable.

ASSATA: Don't be so dramatic. Like I said your spoken English is brilliant. I just don't have the time to be giving you lessons. You have your professors for that.

FANUCO: But they teach in Spanish. And I wanna learn in American.

ASSATA: That's –

FANUCO: I know American is not a language but it's a dream and if you help me improve on my English then I can go and live that dream.

ASSATA: Fanuco, I can't just start giving you lessons. I don't know you from Fanon.

FANUCO: Who?

Can I tell you another reason why you should be my teacher?

ASSATA: Put it in writing.

FANUCO: English or Spanish?

ASSATA: Don't make no difference cause I won't be reading it.

FANUCO: Please, madam.

ASSATA: No, Fanuco. I've made up my mind.

FANUCO: Yes but what does your heart say?

ASSATA: Same thing as my mouth. No!

FANUCO: Just two minutes and I promise I will leave and you shall never see me again.

She lets out a sigh.

ASSATA: This better be good.

FANUCO: If I don't get my English just right then I can kiss my job in Miami goodbye.

She's not convinced.

My uncle and my father haven't always seen eye to eye.

Even when they were younger there has always been this chivalry between them.

ASSATA laughs.

What? Did I say something funny?

Silence.

ASSATA: I think the word you're looking for is rivalry.

FANUCO: So what is chivalry?

ASSATA: Well that died a long time ago so don't you worry yourself about that.

FANUCO: Well there has always been this *rivalry* between my uncle Antonio and my father –

ASSATA: That's all well and good but what's that got to do with me giving you lessons?

FANUCO: I'm getting to it. So what was I saying?

ASSATA: Your father and –

FANUCO: My father doesn't want me to go to Miami.

ASSATA: Well that's your argument dead.

FANUCO: But he's only saying that because of this *rivalry* with uncle Antonio.

Last Tuesday at supper my father said that he will let me go to Miami if I can get the money for the flight and if my English written and spoken improves.

ASSATA: How will he tell if your English has improved?

FANUCO: My uncle told him that he will send me some documents to translate.

Beat

ASSATA: But you will be in Miami you don't need to work on your English. Plenty of Spanish speakers there.

FANUCO: Si. But my father says to me that Uncle Antonio and the Americans will laugh at me if I don't speak English like they do.

ASSATA: Who cares if they laugh at you?

FANUCO: Me.

ASSATA: Why?

FANUCO: Because I want them to respect me. And Americans only respect you when you speak their language.

ASSATA: When will you have time for these lessons? I imagine you're in class all week.

FANUCO: Not on Mondays.

ASSATA: I don't know, Fanuco; Your English is really not that bad.

FANUCO: But you will teach me more than just English.

ASSATA: Like what?

FANUCO: To stand up for myself. Please, madam Assata. I will pay you.

ASSATA: With what money? Do you have a job?

FANUCO: No. I will pay you in... Lo –

ASSATA: If you say Love, I swear I will add to them wounds.

FANUCO: Loyalty.

She takes that in.

ASSATA: How about the flight?

FANUCO: I have some Cucs saved up.

ASSATA: I thought you didn't have a job.

FANUCO: No, this was from last year. I helped my friend Angel sell internet to the tourists. They cannot live without their wifi. *(Mispronounced.)*

ASSATA: Wifi.

FANUCO: To concruz, you should teach me because your lessons will help me prove my father wrong and get me ready for my job on my uncle's farm.

ASSATA: Farm?

FANUCO: He has a criminal law farm in Fort Lauderdale. They deal with – well it's not really anything you'd find interesting.

ASSATA: And how do you know that?

FANUCO: It's all very technical and not as poetical as –

ASSATA: You think I live a solely *poetic* life? Like I don't know about criminals or the law?

FANUCO: Oh I'm not saying that. I mean – *I* find it boring so I don't see how anyone else can enjoy hearing me talk about it.

ASSATA: Then why are you dying to get a job doing something you find boring?

FANUCO: Because I have to.

ASSATA: You don't *have* to do anything you don't want to do.

> *Beat.*

FANUCO: How long have you been in Cuba, madam?

ASSATA: Thirty-two years.

FANUCO: All those years in Cuba and you still don't know that we do what we have to do to stay alive?

ASSATA: I guess you do.

> Firm.

FANUCO: Que?

ASSATA: The word you're looking for is firm not farm. Unless your uncle breeds criminals out there in Fort Laurderdale.

FANUCO: Now you see why I need your help?

So…was the argument strong?

> *She thinks on it.*

ASSATA: Okay, Fanuco. I will teach you.

> *He's beyond excited.*
>
> *He goes to hug her but she blocks him.*
>
> *He opts for a handshake.*

FANUCO: Thank you, madam! I will not let you down.

ASSATA: It's not about me. It's about you and what you need to learn. See you next week Tuesday at 12pm. Goodbye.

> *He almost skips out of the house.*

> *She double locks the door behind him.*

> *She breathes.*

> *She looks to the picture of her grandmother.*

He's a good boy. He just needs a little guidance and I can be that light. No, I doubt it. I like his energy And he sure is funny.

> *With that she turns the music player back on before returning back to her seat with her poetry book.*

> *Once again she breathes.*

SCENE 3

March 22nd 2016

Midday.

ASSATA dances along to some music as she prepares for her first lesson with FANUCO.

A knock is heard faintly. It persists but this time more aggressively.

ASSATA hears the knock at last and turns the music down. She moves to her gun section by the window.

ASSATA: Who is it?

FANUCO: *(Offstage.)* Guess!

> *She sighs.*

> *At the door she finds FANUCO, who stands with sun glasses and a big smile on his face.*

FANUCO: Good afternoon, madam.

ASSATA: Good afternoon, Fanuco.

ASSATA: Come in.

>*He excitedly enters.*

Do you want something to drink?

FANUCO: Some rum.

>*She throws him a 'you must be kidding me' stare.*

But water is better for the heat.

>*She goes to her kitchen area to pour him a glass of water that she hands to him.*

Thank you.

>*She heads back to the kitchen area where she gets a bottle of Havana Club rum – of which she pours a single drop before pouring herself a glass.*

ASSATA: Para los Santos.

>*During the above, FANUCO goes towards the window and makes to open it.*

ASSATA: What are you doing?

FANUCO: Letting in some fresh air.

ASSATA: Did I say you could?

FANUCO: No but I thought –

ASSATA: Stop thinking Fanuco if it's going to make you do stupid things. You don't enter people's homes and start opening their windows. Now step away from the window.

>*He does as told.*

Take out your pen and book.

FANUCO: Yes! Great. Sure. Pen and book.

>*He realises he doesn't even have a bag.*

I forgot.

ASSATA: You forgot?

FANUCO: I forgot.

ASSATA: You're something else, Fanuco Maceo.

FANUCO: I'm sorry, madam. I was just distracted.

ASSATA: Distracted?

FANUCO: Obama.

ASSATA: Obama?

FANUCO: Yes, BARACK HUSSEIN OBAMA was at The Grand Theatre and I was able to see him. It was so exciting. This day will stay with me for the rest of my life. I was even thinking of getting a tattoo; what do you think madam? Should I put March 21st or 21st of March 2016?

> *Short pause.*

ASSATA: Obama visits Cuba and you forget your books and materials.

FANUCO: I couldn't miss this opportunity.

ASSATA: How about the opportunity you are about to miss today?

FANUCO: Pardon?

ASSATA: No materials. No lesson.

FANUCO: I will go back home and bring them.

ASSATA: You will go back home and wait until next week.

FANUCO: Porque?

ASSATA: Because you're clearly not serious about learning.

FANUCO: But… Obama.

ASSATA: What about Obama?

FANUCO: His coolness made me forget.

ASSATA: What is so cool about him?

FANUCO: He's the first black president.

ASSATA: That you know of. There's a whole continent out there that's had black presidents long before Obama even thought of politics.

FANUCO: But Black president in America.

ASSATA: And where are you?

FANUCO: Cuba.

ASSATA: So why do you care about what happens in America?

FANUCO: Because he is black.

ASSATA: And what are you?

FANUCO: I'm black too but I'm not the most powerful man in the world.

ASSATA: How do you expect to walk this world with its fire and thorns if you don't see power in yourself? You may not be the president of the USA but you are alive here and now. You have your own ambitions and dreams so why throw them away because you want a sneak peek at OBAMA?

FANUCO: Didn't you want to see him?

ASSATA: And do what?

FANUCO: Hear him speak.

ASSATA: His words do nothing for me.

FANUCO: How can you not like Obama? He's so cool.

ASSATA: Is that all it takes for you to like someone? Doesn't matter that they're dropping all types of hell on the world.

He's perplexed.

FANUCO: Okay, you ride a difficult bargain.

He gets out a wad of cash – something like 200 Cuban Pesos (National Currency) out of which he takes out a ten peso note.

How does ten peso sound?

ASSATA: Not as sweet as ten Cucs.

FANUCO: Ten Cucs for pen and paper?

ASSATA: Pen and paper that you don't have.

FANUCO: Why do you have to be so – how do I say?

ASSATA: Right?

FANUCO: No. Mean.

ASSATA: Because the world is going to be more than just mean.

FANUCO: Doesn't mean we have to be mean?

ASSATA: Ha ha.

FANUCO: A Pun.

ASSATA: Yes. And it wasn't that bad.

FANUCO: Because I have a great teacher. The best teacher in the whole of Cuba – no, the Caribbean – no, the whole world!

ASSATA: Forget what you've heard, Fanuco. Flattery does NOT get you everywhere.

He drops to his knees.

FANUCO: Oh, Madam. I'm begging you.

ASSATA: And neither does begging. Now go home, Fanuco.

She ushers him out of her house.

He leaves dejected.

A missed opportunity.

I will see you next week same time but with pen and paper.

This lights him up.

He turns to ASSATA with a big smile on his face.

FANUCO: Thank you, Madam Assata. See you next week.

He exits closing the door behind him.

She follows behind and double locks it.

She goes to her Grandma's picture. She picks it up and takes it to her rocking chair where she takes a seat.

ASSATA: He learned something today. Might not be what he wanted but it was what he needed to learn. He's gotta start taking himself seriously or no one else will. Meet with Obama? And say what? Take me off the list? Why did you double the price on my head? Let me come home? He do what a president do. Don't you worry, I will be alright. Love you too.

She gets up and returns the picture to its usual place.

She takes in a deep breath that she lets out slowly. At peace.

SCENE 4

March 29th 2016

FANUCO sits at the table with ASSATA standing next to him; His essay in her hand.

ASSATA: What kind of argument is this?

Now, your professor asked you to convince her that going to the US was better than staying in Cuba. All you did was say that you were going. It's sad that your father is ill and that your mother has to look after him but I don't think it's strong enough. And to top it off you didn't do it in an interesting way. It was all very elementary.

FANUCO: What does elementary mean?

ASSATA: Basic. Fanuco, you write like a child.

FANUCO: But I *am* a child.

ASSATA: No, you are a man, Fanuco. A well spoken man with the writing style of a three year old.

Now you say your father is ill.

FANUCO: Yes.

ASSATA: How is that relevant to the essay?

FANUCO: Relevant?

ASSATA: As in, what has that go to do with what your professor asked?

FANUCO: Because he's the man of the house. If he's ill then he cannot work and if he cannot work then we cannot eat and if we cannot eat then –

ASSATA: Then you can't survive.

FANUCO: I was going to say live. But survive is a better word.

He writes it down.

ASSATA: What's wrong with him?

FANUCO: We don't know but he is feeling tired a lot.

ASSATA: Has he gone to a doctor?

FANUCO: My father doesn't believe in Cuban Doctors. He says the bad pay is all they can think about. So he's gone to a Santero for a consulta.

ASSATA: And what did they say?

FANUCO: They said he should rest and beware of pain in his house. Now he thinks that I am the pain.

ASSATA: I can see why he would think that.

FANUCO: Ouch.

Beat

ASSATA: Rhetoric. Do you know what that means?

FANUCO: Retorica? Si. The art of persecution – no persuasion.

ASSATA: And what are the three elements that make up rhetoric?

FANUCO: Umm.

ASSATA: Umm? I don't remember Umm being one of them.

FANUCO: In Spanish or English?

ASSATA: You choose.

FANUCO: Logotipos, caracter distintivo, patetismo.

ASSATA: Logos, Ethos and Pathos. And what do they all represent?

He's struggling with the translation.

FANUCO: Logos; make a reasonable argument? Ethos; your character that makes you the right person to make the argument?; Pathos; the way you make the audience feel after your speech or argument?

ASSATA: There's little evidence of any of that in your essay.

FANUCO: Logos, I live in Havana; Ethos, I live in Havana and Pathos, I live in HAVANA!

ASSATA: It's no wonder I loathed what you wrote.

FANUCO: Loathed?

ASSATA: Yes, as in I thought it was so terrible that I felt a pain in my stomach.

FANUCO: But at least you felt something.

ASSATA: But it's the bad kind of something.

FANUCO: Something is better than nothing.

ASSATA: So you are a little Mr Know-it-all, hunh?

FANUCO: Not at all, Madam Assata. There's so much that I don't know.

Beat.

ASSATA: You said your mother isn't working.

FANUCO: Did I?

ASSATA: Yes in your "assignment".

FANUCO: Oh yes, she was working for Banco Financiero but she had to leave when my father got sick.

ASSATA: Alright I guess it's perfect for the pathos part of the argument. Why don't you work out how to include that in a concise way that shows that you would be better off living in Miami with your uncle.

He writes down her advice.

FANUCO: You know what, madam sometimes I wish The Obamas was my parents.

ASSATA: The Obamas? The Obamas have their own family and worries.

FANUCO: But they don't have a son. I would be a great son to Michelle and Barack.

ASSATA: Worry about being a great son to your own parents.

FANUCO: But I cannot be in this country any longer!

ASSATA: The man in the water wants to be in the clouds and the man in the clouds wants to be in the water. But what happens when they get to where they want and find that the clouds are just as cold and the water as dangerous?

FANUCO: Is that what you call a…metaphor?

ASSATA: It's what I call reality. Right now you are in a fantasy.

FANUCO: I like Fantasy.

ASSATA: But fantasy will drive you mad because it doesn't match with your reality.

FANUCO: But I don't like my reality. I want to do something to change it but I can't.

ASSATA: And why can't you?

FANUCO: Because I am not rich.

ASSATA: Do you know the true definition of rich?

FANUCO: Rico. Mucho dinero!

ASSATA: I can't teach you how to be rich if rich means having "mucho dinero".

FANUCO: So what does it mean?

ASSATA: It means living the kind of life that lets other people in, help them move up. When you've got a lot of money, like you say you want, you may feel the urge to push people out and kick them down where you think they belong.

FANUCO: I'm not trying to kick anyone down.

ASSATA: You're leaving your family here and going up to Miami.

FANUCO: Because there I can make money.

ASSATA: Crumbs.

FANUCO: Collect enough crumbs and one day I can have my own loaf.

ASSATA: Stay here and you can share that loaf with your family.

> *Fair point.*

Where's *your* family?

ASSATA: Here.

FANUCO: Can I meet them?

ASSATA: You already have?

FANUCO: When?

She points at him.

He turns around to where the gods are.

These?

ASSATA: No. You.

FANUCO: I'm not your family.

ASSATA: Yes you are.

FANUCO: But we only met two weeks ago.

ASSATA: Do you know what family means?

FANUCO: Yes, like mother, father, sister, uncle.

ASSATA: And what am I to you?

FANUCO: My teacher?

ASSATA: Fanuco, You don't know that in Africa the women in your village are your mothers, the men your fathers, the boys your brothers and girls your sisters.

See you can't walk this land thinking that only those in your house are your family. You look like me, and I look like you. You are my family. It's why I couldn't walk by as those boys beat you like that.

Now that you know you are my son and I am your mother we have to act accordingly. You have to love me and I have to love you. I must empower you with honesty, support and encouragement and punish you when you step out of line and you must respect me, take care of me, and make me proud. You ask me where's my family? It's right here. In Cuba.

FANUCO: Madam, we are not in Africa and me and you are not African.

ASSATA: I was hoping you would be smarter than that, Fanuco.

Where do you think, Oshun, Shango and Yemaya are from?

FANUCO: They are just Santeria gods. Not African gods.

ASSATA: What makes you think that?

FANUCO: Because the white Cubans pray to them too.

Short pause.

ASSATA: I wonder what your great grandfather would say if he heard you say that you are not African.

FANUCO: What does it matter? He was not a General for the Angolan or Nigerian Army. He fought for Cuba. Fidel is more African than him.

ASSATA: Where do you think Antonio Maceo's ancestors came from? Like it or not, Fanuco. You are African.

FANUCO: Madam, I came for English lessons. Not lessons on Africa.

ASSATA: You about the dumbest fool I ever met! You come to me saying you want to know about everything to do with America. Cause you love America. Well how you think America got so loveable? Off the blood and sweat of those same Africans you deny. You think you just magically appeared in Cuba? You had to have come from somewhere and it wasn't Miami. It was Africa. You are African.

Say it.

FANUCO: What?

ASSATA: Say you are African.

FANUCO: Madam, what's wrong with you?

ASSATA: Ain't nothing wrong me? It's you that's in the wrong. Talking about you ain't African. With beautiful dark skin like that, boy you got to be African!

FANUCO: But people call me –

ASSATA: Forget what they call you and listen to what I say to you. You are African. Now say it.

FANUCO: *(Unconvincingly)* I am African.

ASSATA: Say it like you got sugar cane on your tongue.

FANUCO: I am African! I am African!! I AM AFRICAN!

ASSATA: That's it. That's it. Now we're getting somewhere.

Okay, Fanuco Maceo, great grandson of Antonio Maceo, African, Bronze Titan, hero of the Revolution. That's enough work for today. See you again next week.

FANUCO: Thank you, madam.

> *He packs his work away and heads for the exit.*
>
> *ASSATA watches him leave before double locking her door.*
>
> *She looks to her Grandma.*

ASSATA: He had to say it. That way he can taste how good it sounds. You wanna hear something funny, Grandma? When he said those beautiful words, it reminded me of Fred. You remember, Fred? Fred Hampton? The revolutionary brother from the Chicago chapter? Well this boy is a Revolutionary too. He just don't know it yet. But he will.

If I got anything to do with it.

> *With that she throws a smile to her Grandma before turning the lights off.*

SCENE 5

April 26th 2016

A month later.

Evening.

ASSATA is marking one of FANUCO's essays.

We hear the heavy patter of rain outside.

She sits. Agitated.

An aggressive knock.

She gets a gun from behind the door and holds it à la Malcolm X at the window.

ASSATA: Who is it?

FANUCO: It's me, Madam.

> *She hurriedly puts the gun away before opening for the young man who stands there dripping wet from the rain. She pulls him in.*

FANUCO: I'm sorry, Madam Assata but I cannot have our lesson today.

ASSATA: You keep me waiting for hours just to tell me that?

FANUCO: I'm sorry, Madam.

ASSATA: No, Fanuco. Sorry is not enough. I'm doing this for you. How do you except anyone to take you seriously if you play around with your future? It's you that begged me to teach you.

FANUCO: My father is dead.

> *Short pause.*

I had to wait with my sister and mother until the doctor came.

> *Short pause.*

ASSATA: *(Offstage.)* I'm sorry, Fanuco.

FANUCO: Why? You didn't kill him.

ASSATA: Still. I'm sorry.

Come in.

FANUCO: I have to go back and –

ASSATA: No. Let me at least give you a change of clothes.

> *He stands there dejected as she goes to get him a towel and a change of clothes.*
>
> *He stands in stillness.*
>
> *After a while she returns with dry clothes and a towel.*

Here.

> *He goes to get changed there.*

Don't be silly, Fanuco go and change in the bathroom.

> *He drags his feet to the bathroom.*
>
> *ASSATA gets a rug and cleans up the rain water on the floor. As she's done FANUCO enters and loiters by the bathroom door.*

Take a seat. Let me get you a hot drink.

FANUCO: Have you got anything stronger?

> *She thinks on it before exiting.*
>
> *FANUCO again, stands in stillness.*
>
> *He then starts to cry hands in face.*
>
> *ASSATA returns with a new bottle of Havana Club rum.*
>
> *She gets two glasses.*
>
> *She watches him crying – unsure what to do.*
>
> *She opens the bottle and pours libation.*

ASSATA: Para Los Santos.

She pours two glasses one of which she hands FANUCO.

He takes the glass of rum from her hand and downs it.

ASSATA: Take it easy, Fanuco.

FANUCO: It's hard to take it easy when you've never had it that way.

ASSATA: You must stay strong, Fanuco. Okay? For your mother and sister.

FANUCO: How can I when my father has died?

ASSATA: Tell what me happened.

Pause.

FANUCO: He died in his sleep. He refused to go to the doctors and wouldn't even let them treat him at home. He spent the little money we had on the Santeros and all they could give him was words. Like you! All you have is words!

ASSATA: That's it, let all out.

FANUCO: Don't tell me what I should do. I will let out what I want!

ASSATA: That's it.

He then starts to throw all types of obscenities but in Spanish.

FANUCO: *I wasted my time here with you you old bitch when I could have been looking after my father.*

Translation: Perra vieja, perdí mi tiempo contigo cuando podría haber estado cuidando de mi padre!

ASSATA replies in Spanish too.

ASSATA: *Your father would have died whether you stayed by his side or not.*

Tu padre habría muerto de todos modos.

He's back to English.

FANUCO: But I could have been there. I could have actually been able to help. All he needed was his son.

ASSATA: All he needed was to go and see a doctor.

Don't start blaming yourself.

FANUCO: What else can I do? I can't bring him back.

ASSATA: And you think blaming yourself will make him rise from the dead?

Beat.

FANUCO: Before he died...he asked me to promise him that I would look after my ma and my sister. But how can I do that?

ASSATA: Support them.

FANUCO: Support them with what? Empty hands?

ASSATA: Make sure you're there when they need you.

FANUCO: You are trying to do that not direct – indirect thing.

You don't want me to leave Cuba.

ASSATA: Not now. Not when your family need you the most.

FANUCO lets out a harsh scream.

FANUCO: I don't want be in this country anymore! I want to go to America! I want American dollars not Pesos or Cucs!

I want my father back, Assata! Are you going to bring him back? Or are you going to teach more metaphors and puns? Can I give metaphors and puns to my mother and sister to eat? I want to have money! Money that matters. I'm not even learning anything. You are a terrible teacher, Assata.

ASSATA: I know you're grieving but don't you dare say my name with all that venom in your mouth. You know what it means? It means I struggle for my people. Don't tell me that I am a terrible teacher. You don't know who I am.

Almost face to face with ASSATA.

FANUCO: Do you know me?

Pause.

ASSATA: I know you are a child. Because children are the ones who start crying when things don't turn out like the cartoons.

You thought the world would be easy? Ha! Run away from Cuba and go to America but life is going to be hard wherever you go. You cannot bring back your father but you can continue to love your mother and sister so focus on that.

FANUCO sits down on the floor.

ASSATA joins him.

FANUCO: I cannot stay here. My mother expects so much now. I need to step up. The job with my uncle is me stepping up.

ASSATA: Why don't you ask *him* to help?

FANUCO: My mother's pride will not allow it. But Madam if you lend me the money for the flight to Miami, I will pay you back.

ASSATA: What happened to the little Cucs you had saved up?

FANUCO: My father spent them on the Santeros.

ASSATA: Something don't make sense to me, Fanuco. Your uncle Antonio owns this law firm, has a job ready for you where I imagine he will have to pay you a wage and now you're telling me that he can't afford to throw you some travel money?

FANUCO: You make it sound like I'm lying to you.

ASSATA: I didn't say anything about lies. It just doesn't make sense.

FANUCO: A flight to Fort lauderdale costs over a $100. American. Tell me madam, when you have your own family to feed and a business that is hardly making enough money to keep the lights on – do you think you can afford to throw travel money to your hated dead brother's son?

ASSATA: I guess you don't. But how will he pay for your wages?

FANUCO: He said I will get what I put in. So with each client I help him get, I will receive a commission.

ASSATA: Brutal.

FANUCO: Commission is better than nothing. I just need the money to get there.

ASSATA gets up.

ASSATA: And you want me to give you all the money you need. Me the "terrible" teacher.

He gets up too.

FANUCO: I didn't mean that. I was angry. I will pay you back, madam.

ASSATA: I would rather you stay so we finish what we started. You've picked up everything I've taught you so quickly but there's so much more you've yet to learn.

FANUCO: Miami is not that far. You can come and we have our lessons there.

ASSATA: Fanuco, you must think I have money to burn. Over the past month I have given up hour after hour to teach you and now you're just going to up and leave?

I can't give you the money, Fanuco.

He's heartbroken.

I'm sorry.

Pause.

FANUCO surveys the house before taking his attention to the clothes he has on.

FANUCO: You just have spare men's clothes that fit me lying around?

ASSATA: What do you mean?

FANUCO: Whose are these?

ASSATA: You're not the only person I know, Fanuco.

FANUCO: Do all the people you know leave their clothes here?

ASSATA: What are you saying?

He approaches her.

FANUCO: I know all about you, Assata.

ASSATA: Ain't nothing wrong with that.

FANUCO: I know what Americans like you want.

He starts to undress.

I will do what it takes to get to America.

She gently helps him put his clothes back.

ASSATA: Go home to your mother and sister.

She delicately ushers him towards the front door where she gives him an umbrella before he exits.

ASSATA goes to double lock the door.

She looks in the direction of her Grandma's picture.

She rushes to her bedroom.

ACT TWO

SCENE 1

May 2nd 2016

ASSATA stands as though in a trance.

The knock on the door snaps her out of it.

ASSATA: Who is it?!

FANUCO: *(Offstage.)* Madam? Madam. It's Fanuco.

ASSATA: Fanuco?

What are you doing here?

> *She lets him in before shutting and double locking the door.*

> *He has his back pack on his back and carries the umbrella ASSATA gave him.*

FANUCO: I came to…I would like – I would like to apologise. I wasn't feeling like myself and I was wrong for doing what I did last week.

> *Short pause.*

ASSATA: Fanuco, you gon' be the death of me if you not careful. I'm too old to be fretting over a boy that don't respect me but expect me to bend over backwards just so he can learn.

FANUCO: I do respect you, madam.

ASSATA: Respect ain't in no words. It's in how you treat the people in your life, how you appreciate them.

FANUCO: I do appreciate you, madam.

ASSATA: There you go with them words again, boy. You just throw them together and hope they stick.

She's overcome with emotion. Tries not to let the tears fall. FANUCO notices.

FANUCO: Madam, are you okay?

ASSATA: No. No, I am not.

FANUCO: What's wrong?

Pause.

ASSATA: I'm not who you think I am.

FANUCO: What does that mean?

ASSATA: You need me to teach you everything? What do you think it means?

FANUCO: That you have been lying to me?

ASSATA: I wouldn't go that far. I just haven't told you certain things.

FANUCO: Like what?

Pause.

ASSATA: Tupac Shakur.

A glint in his eyes.

FANUCO: Yes?

ASSATA: Well he was my Godson.

FANUCO: Tupac was your Godson?!

ASSATA: Yes and his mother, Afeni who was like a sister to me, passed away last night.

You know what passed away means?

FANUCO: She died.

I am sorry to hear that.

ASSATA: You got nothing to be sorry for. She's now resting in power. I just wish I had seen her one last time. You know

33

Fanuco, to be strong sometimes is to let yourself be weak. And today I don't think I can give you our usual lesson.

FANUCO: Madam. I don't know if you've realised but our lessons so far have been very unusual.

He takes his bag off before placing the umbrella to one side.

Let me get you something to drink.

ASSATA: Oh, Fanuco. You ain't gotta do that.

FANUCO: I want to, Madam.

He exits to the kitchen.

We watch ASSATA swaying back and forth.

She quietly sings to herself.

ASSATA: Oh, sister, Afeni, I pray you went peacefully. I know, now you join your young cub. Give me the strength to keep struggling because my heart aches, sister. It aches from the blood that no longer pumps through ever since I left. But it also yearns for the days when we were active – dismantling their racist system so much they threw everything they could at us.

I know it feel like I'm here in sunny Cuba, Havana club flowing down my throat but I wanna be there; boots strapped, locs flowing, with a semi-automatic pointed to the heavens; I wanna be in Ferguson; I wanna be there with them all side by side; I wanna be there to speak to the families of brother Eric, brother Freddie, sister Sandra, the young babies Trayvon, Tamir, Aiyana and everyone who's had their breath taken when all they were trying to do is live!

I guess they like the colour of our blood more than they love the colour of our skin; Why else they wanna see it flow from our bodies?

She screams.

She starts to move around.

FANUCO enters as she's moving manically.

I, Assata Olugbala Shakur continue the struggle for my
people. My veins are filled with African blood so you
know I'm a warrior; You know I am fighter. They had
my ancestors in chains, thinking they could keep them
down but they rose up because that's what we do. We
get stronger with each struggle they throw our way. They
don't know it but I sense a powerful tide coming. These
young ones, warrior sister, Afeni! They feel the fire we lit
for them. They feel it from Baltimore, Paris to London and
it burns bright. So bright it's no wonder their eyes are red
with anger.

She spots FANUCO.

Fanuco, come join me in a dance.

She puts some music on.

FANUCO: I'm not really a dancer, madam.

ASSATA: Don't you worry. I will lead.

FANUCO: But the man is supposed to lead.

ASSATA: You leave your misogyny at the door when you enter
my house! You hear?!

FANUCO: Yes, madam.

ASSATA: Now put the tray down and join me.

> *She doesn't even wait for him to place the tray down. It
> almost spills.*
>
> *They start to dance. It's really fast paced.*
>
> *ASSATA leads and gradually FANUCO finds his groove.*
>
> *They are enjoying themselves.*
>
> *The song changes to something slower.*

FANUCO goes to sit back down but ASSATA holds onto him.

They sway gently.

ASSATA: Fanuco. Hold me, I feel like I'm about to fall.

FANUCO hugs his crying teacher. It lasts for a short while before FANUCO takes his teacher by the hands.

FANUCO: You gotta stay strong, Madam. It's easy to sit there and cry all day but it's not going to help.

The other day for the first time me and my mother spoke. But I don't mean speak like "hi how are you?" I mean we spoke like two human beings. Not mother and son.

You see, my mother has always seen me as a baby even though I am the eldest.

There is no difference to the way she speaks to me and the way she speaks to Celia.

And I make it worse. I lose all the bass in my voice whenever I speak to her. It must be because I feel like I am in trouble when she calls my name. When she asks me to do something. I feel like she's trying to catch me out. But after we buried my father, we spoke.

And we cried.

So Madam Assata it's okay.

Everything is going to be fine.

ASSATA: Thank you, baby.

She kisses him on the cheek.

FANUCO: What was she like?

Pause.

ASSATA: Strong. Powerful. Gentle. Just like her son.

Silence.

FANUCO: Will you be going to her funeral?

ASSATA: No.

FANUCO: Why not?

ASSATA: It's not possible. I have unfinished business here.

FANUCO: What can be more important that saying goodbye to your sister, madam?

ASSATA: You. When I agree to something, I stick to it.

FANUCO: Madam, I give you official permission to go to America and say good bye to your sister.

She puts a hand to his cheek.

ASSATA: Haha, that's very sweet, Fanuco. But you don't have that kind of jurisdiction. It's okay. My daughter will be there on my behalf.

FANUCO: You have a daughter?

ASSATA: Yes, I do. Kakuya. My rock.

FANUCO: Well I don't know if I could have missed my father's funeral. He probably would have jumped out of the grave and beat me for not going.

ASSATA: You miss him don't you?

Beat.

FANUCO: I used to want my father to hurry up and die. That way I can get on and be who I want to be without feeling him judging me. But now that he's gone I want nothing more than to see him again. He used to sing a song that made my mother smile. He always sung it around the house. If we heard him sing it we knew it would be a great day. You want to hear it?

ASSATA: I would love to.

She sits.

FANUCO sings an Africanised version of Guantanamera using Jose Marti's Poem.

It's sweet.

Brings tears to ASSATA's eyes (and ours).

FANUCO: Guantanamera, Guantanamera.
Guantanamera, Guantanamera.

Yo soy un hombre sincero, de donde crece la palma.
Yo soy un hombre sincero, de donde crece la palma.
Y antes de morir yo quiero cantar mis versos del alma.
Guantanamera, Guantanamera.
Guantanamera, Guantanamera.

Translation: I am a truthful man; I come from where the palm tree grows, I am a trueed man, who comes from where the palm trees grow, Before I lay down my life, I long to coin the verses of my soul.

ASSATA: You must teach me that some time.

FANUCO: Why sometime? Why not this time?

And it's easy. You must have heard it before.

ASSATA: I have but I've never heard it sung like that before.

FANUCO: My father always took famous songs and made them African.

ASSATA: Everything sounds beautiful once you add Africa to it. But I don't want to ruin your father's song.

FANUCO: No, madam. It's not my father's song, it's Cuba's song.

Plus, you have a beautiful voice. It will put a smile on my face if you sang it with me.

ASSATA: But I have tears in my voice it won't sound as good.

FANUCO: The more tears in your voice the better. Come on.

FANUCO sings the first Guantanemara before ASSATA joins in with a harmony.

They follow the same pattern for the verse before singing the second refrain together.

It sounds beautiful and fills the place almost like a choir in a church.

Pause.

FANUCO: My mother thinks that my father died of a broken heart.

Pause.

ASSATA: Why does she think that?

FANUCO: Because he couldn't even afford food for his family.

ASSATA: Hunh.

FANUCO: It's true.

He never looked us in the eye when he spoke. He talked so quietly even *he* couldn't hear himself.

Sometimes he floated through the house like he was a dead man with no life in his body. He was dead long before he left us. But he was my father.

He is on the verge of tears.

ASSATA: Fanuco.

FANUCO: I wrote something last night, madam. Would you like to hear it?

ASSATA: Sure.

He goes into his bag and takes out his notepad.

FANUCO: Cuba destroyed my father. She made him go mad. He put his soul in her hands and she threw it on the ground and watched it melt. I cannot turn into him. I cannot follow a dead man's footsteps. Because I know where he's leading me. There's a grave out there with my name on it but I don't want it to be in Cuba. She's beautiful, she has my heart but she don't know how to love us.

Pause.

You didn't like it.

ASSATA: I don't have to like it. I just need to believe in what you're saying.

FANUCO: And did you?

ASSATA: Ask yourself that.

FANUCO: Yes. I did.

ASSATA: Then how can I not?

FANUCO: Wow. Thank you. That means a lot.

ASSATA: Was that your goodbye letter to Cuba?

FANUCO: More of a love letter.

ASSATA: Sounded like you were breaking up with her.

FANUCO: Like I said, she don't know how to love and she's not giving me what I want, madam.

ASSATA: But aren't you getting what you *need?*

FANUCO: I'm not even getting that.

ASSATA: You must be getting something.

FANUCO: I'm getting nothing madam. Nothing!

ASSATA: Change your tone.

FANUCO: What tone? I'm not shouting.

ASSATA: I don't have the strength to fight you today.

FANUCO: Who said anything about fights?!

ASSATA: I won't tell you again, Fanuco. Change. Your. Tone.

He's now face to face with her.

FANUCO: Stop telling me what to do?

When you said you that you wouldn't give me the money
I needed, I thought I would put America to bed. So, I went
to find some work. I tried restaurants, hotels, restaurants in
hotels, I even offered to clean but they all said no.

I've always thought that if I stayed obedient, did what
I was told then I will get what I deserve. A great job, a
loving family and respect. But I'm learning that's not how
the world works.

ASSATA: My work here is done.

FANUCO: You're making jokes madam but I'm being serious.

ASSATA: You don't know how easy you have it.

FANUCO: Then why does easy hurt so much?

ASSATA: I am grieving, Fanuco.

FANUCO: And you think I'm not? I lost my father – all you
lost was your warrior sister – whatever that means. He was
my flesh and blood, she just helped you shed some blood.

ASSATA: And you are making mine boil, boy.

FANUCO: At last! You will put away with these words then we
will see who you really are. Human. You are allowed to get
angry, madam. It won't make you weak.

ASSATA: You think I give a fuck about what you think of me?!
Young man I have fought more pigs, wolves and monsters
than you could ever dream of! I *am* strength. Whether I be
crying or whooping your ass.

FANUCO: You threatening me madam?

ASSATA: I'm way too smart for threats.

FANUCO: I know people. And they ain't no wordsmiths.

Long pause as ASSATA looks at FANUCO. She's hurt.

ASSATA: Once upon a time –

FANUCO: I'm not in the mood for your fairy tales.

ASSATA: This ain't no fairy tale, so shut up and listen.

Once upon a time in America, killing black people was so much fun that some of the white people in the town would gather around, even bring a snack or two, along with their kids, to watch a black man or woman being lynched.

The thing with lynching, you need a strong sturdy tree. One with firm roots. Then you need a rope. It too needs to be strong. You tie the rope up into a noose as so.

She shows the noose she's made out of an Aux cable.

Then you find yourself what they call a nigger. In those days, any would do. Put said noose around this particular nigger.

She goes to put the noose around FANUCO's neck who stands there in shock.

FANUCO: What are you doing?

He relents.

ASSATA: I haven't got a tree so I guess this will do.

She throws the other end of the rope over a piece of overhead wood that makes up part of the ceiling.

FANUCO: Madam. I get it.

ASSATA: I don't want you to get it. I want you to *feel* it.

Now that the noose is around the nigger and firmly in place, you look to make sure your invited audience is watching. Then you pull like this.

She pulls the rope. FANUCO starts to rise up his hand on the noose around his neck.

FANUCO: Madam.

ASSATA: You pull until the feet are off the ground.

FANUCO: Madam…please.

ASSATA: Once the feet are off the ground you hold. You hold until the nigger starts to beg for his life. Till all the faeces escape him till the life is choked out of him.

FANUCO: Madam – mmadam. STOP!! I feel it. I feel it. I feel it. I feel it.

> *He repeats this as he's lowered.*
>
> *We slowly fade to black.*

ACT THREE

May 9th 2016

Evening.

ASSATA in her room.

Knock Knock.

She enters from her bedroom.

She goes towards the window where she hides her gun and makes to draw for it.

ASSATA: Who is it?

FANUCO: *(Offstage.)* It's me.

> *She goes to open.*

> *At the door, she finds FANUCO.*

ASSATA: Good evening, Fanuco.

FANUCO: Good evening, madam.

> *He stays at the door.*

ASSATA: You've come back?

FANUCO: Yes.

ASSATA: Well come in.

> *He enters.*

Take a seat.

> *He goes to sit.*

You hungry?

She makes to exit.

FANUCO: Why did you have to do that?

This stops her in her tracks.

ASSATA: You had to feel what I was saying.

FANUCO: You couldn't give me a lecture like other teachers?

ASSATA: I'm not like other teachers.

FANUCO: You were ready to kill me just to teach me a lesson?; just so I could feel what you're saying?

ASSATA: You weren't gonna die. Stop being so dramatic.

FANUCO: You hang your student from a ceiling and I'm being dramatic. You will have to look for a new definition for dramatic.

ASSATA: I will do whatever it takes for you to get the tools to survive this world.

FANUCO: Even if it kills me?

ASSATA: Even if it kills you.

FANUCO: Why are you even here?

What are you hiding, madam?

ASSATA: Don't play dumb. It's not cute.

FANUCO: I am not trying to be cute. I'm trying to be smart and I want to know more about YOU.

ASSATA: Everything you need to know about me is out there. You just have to go investigate.

With that she exits to the kitchen.

FANUCO takes off his bag and opens it. He checks to see where ASSATA is. He hears her singing in the kitchen.

He slowly takes out a piece of paper.

It's a wanted poster of ASSATA SHAKUR. He looks at it. Scrutinizes it then places it in his pocket.

He then takes out of his bag a pistol that he holds in shaky hands.

We hear ASSATA's voice coming closer.

He quickly shoves the gun at the back of his trousers.

ASSATA returns with Tostones.

Brought you something sweet.

FANUCO: Thank you.

ASSATA: So, how was your week?

FANUCO: It was good.

ASSATA: I'm sure you can find a better word than "good".

FANUCO: It was terrifically incredible.

ASSATA: You're never going to expand on your vocabulary if use such simplistic adjectives.

FANUCO: Ayayayai, all you asked me was how my week was. I didn't think it was a test.

ASSATA: I'm not testing you, Fanuco. I just need you to understand the importance of language. The way you speak says a lot about who you are and your intentions.

FANUCO: Okay. I had a very…investigative week. I came across a word that has been confusing me.

ASSATA: What is it?

FANUCO: Terr –

No it's a stupid word.

ASSATA: No such thing as stupid words.

Pause.

FANUCO: What is a *terrorist?*

> *She lets that land.*

ASSATA: What a word.

Well a terrorist is an individual who commits politically motivated violence in a clandestine manner against non-combatants in order to create a fearful state of mind in a group of people different from the victims.

FANUCO: ???

ASSATA: Someone who hurts or kills innocent people in order to scare others.

FANUCO: Like you?

> *Silence.*
>
> *He takes out the wanted poster and places it on the table.*
>
> *She takes the poster, scrutinizes it. She smiles.*

ASSATA: Hunh. America's Most Wanted

FANUCO: See I've been spending all this time with you. I have even seen you more than I have seen my own mother.

Last week got me thinking. What kind of teacher tries to lynch her own student? So I went out there and started asking questions. But the answers have been right there. Under my nose. You're Tupac's Godmother!

People know you, Assata Shakur.

The rappers, rastas, even my uncle.

Then I started to wonder, why didn't I know about you?

Why has it taken me this long to know the real you?

ASSATA: You haven't always been the brightest bulb.

FANUCO: There goes the metaphors. You should be proud of me.

47

ASSATA: I've always been proud of you, Fanuco.

FANUCO: Wait till you hear what I have to say. You might not be proud anymore.

ASSATA: I know exactly what you're going to say. Same thing I've been hearing for the past forty years.

Same thing the oppressors stateside say. You're gonna say *I* am a terrorist. Because it's what you've been told.

Now, do you think a country that kills innocent people all year round has any right to call anyone else a terrorist?

FANUCO: You killed a man.

> *She approaches him.*
>
> *She stands before him takes his hand and places it below her underarm.*

ASSATA: Feel that.

> *He feels under her arm.*

Tell me how I could have found the strength to lift up a gun and shoot someone with a bullet lodged under my arm and another having passed through my back?

> *ASSATA returns to her seat.*

Take your pen and paper out and let us start our lesson.

> *It looks like he's about to yield.*

FANUCO: Why do they say you murdered someone when you didn't?

ASSATA: Fear.

They feared that people were starting to awake from their slumber of oppression and relate to what black revolutionaries like myself were teaching them; Stop feeding the fat capitalist cats. They *feared* a liberated Black people.

FANUCO: Why would they fear that when America is the "land of the free and home of the –

ASSATA: Murderers on a police payroll? You know what ubiquitous means?

FANUCO: Yes.

ASSATA: Well so you will know that in Cuba I feel free wherever I go. The minute I step foot on U.S soil… I will be free no more.

FANUCO: But, if you are a black revolutionary I'm sure that you have supporters.

ASSATA: Of course I have supporters but I also have enemies. And right now my enemies have all the power.

FANUCO: Then go and take it from them! You think if you stay in Cuba you're getting your power?

You think we can continue to house a fugitive who stands between us and a better standard of life?

Why should *we* starve trying to keep *you* free? Freedom costs money.

He takes the gun from his hip/lower back and points it at ASSATA.

And this is how I plan to pay for mine.

ASSATA: Fanuco! Where did you get that?

FANUCO: I told you. I know people.

ASSATA: Do you know what you are doing?

FANUCO: Yes. I do.

Now get up.

ASSATA: Fanuco, no.

FANUCO: Get up.

ASSATA: Fanuco put the gun –

FANUCO: GET. UP!

> *She slowly acquiesces.*

ASSATA: What do you think is going to happen?

FANUCO: They say, $2m for the safe return of JoAnne Chesimard. I plan on making sure you are safely returned, JoAnne so I can get my $2m.

ASSATA: Then all your problems will go away, right?

FANUCO: Yes.

ASSATA: And where will you live? In the States? Where a *woman* or *child* can frighten a grown man so much that he shoots to kill?

What do you think they will do to *you*, Big Bad Black man with what looks like a gun in his hand?

> *He ponders on this. Doesn't care. Continues to move her to the door.*

And you definitely can't live here no more.

> *They stop.*

FANUCO: Why not? This is my home. If America won't have me then my Cuba will.

ASSATA: You really think you will be able to walk these streets as the boy who killed a revolutionary?

FANUCO: You're not a revolutionary! You're a fugitive! A terrorist and a traitor to your struggle. You say you want to liberate black people then start with yourself.

How can you be free here? You're in hiding from the big bad Americans. What kind of free woman couldn't even go to her "sister's" funeral!

> *That catches ASSATA.*

She turns away from him as though she's about to get shot in the back.

ASSATA: My grandmother has always had these dreams but this one really excited her. She dreamed that she was dressing me. I asked her why was she dressing me, was I little?

And she said no, I was grown. Now I'm starting to get scared because unless I couldn't use my arms, only reason she would dress me is if I was dead. But she assured me I was alive. She told me not to get too used to that prison, that I will get out soon.

She turns to face him.

Fanuco, I have the same dream for you.

All this is temporary. You're a special case because you were born free, true to your name, Fanuco. I was born a slave in America. Caged in their twentieth century plantations.

I chose to come here to get my freedom but you enslaved yourself in a free land. But don't you get too used to that prison.

Now why don't you put the gun down, take a seat and let's continue with our lesson.

She extends her hand out.

Fanuco. Fanuco.

FANUCO gently puts the gun down. ASSATA takes it from him, takes out the magazine and dismantles the gun impressively.

FANUCO: I have done something bad, madam.

ASSATA: You did what you thought you had to do.

FANUCO: But I didn't have to.

ASSATA: It's okay we've resolved it.

FANUCO: But I have done something worse.

ASSATA: What do you mean?

FANUCO: ...I knew I wouldn't have the heart to do this so I spoke to my uncle. And he called some of his friends in Old Havana.

ASSATA: Fanuco! What have you done?

FANUCO: I'm sorry madam but you should leave.

ASSATA: How many times do I have to tell you? I will not be leaving CUBA! This is my home! No one can ever get me to leave. Not you, not your uncle and not them racist pigs!

She starts to check behind her window.

Takes out her gun.

If they think I'm going quietly then they obviously don't know that I am a warrior!

FANUCO: You don't know these men, Madam!

ASSATA: What's there to know? They want to kill me and I want live. So I defend myself.

FANUCO: When I see you like this, madam. I start to wonder.

ASSATA: You better start wondering whether you're gonna stay or leave.

FANUCO: But this is my family. I can't stay and fight them.

ASSATA: Those are not your family! Anyone who wants to kill their own cannot be family.

FANUCO: But you killed another human being.

ASSATA: I did not kill anyone! Why do you keep saying that?

They've been killing me since I was born. They come and stop me and my brothers, ask us to put our hands up and commence to carry out a northern lynching. Shoot me Point Blank and I take the blame for their incompetence?

Because they couldn't kill me they tried to find other ways to end my life; Stop me from living.

She's really breaking now.

Even now forty years later and they still call me a murderer. They drown my name in blood and it's them who are steeped in it.

They lock up my whole family, Mumia, Sundiata, Geronimo, all our comrades. They even have you locked up and you don't even know it. I took my freedom, freed myself and they still chasing me with them hounds, teeth out salivating for my flesh and blood. Well they ain't coming for me. Cause I'm ready this time.

If I am a murderer then what are they? What's Nixon, Hoover, Heisenhower, Reagan, Bush Sr, Bush Jr? Even your beloved Obama.

But *I* am a murderer?!

I'm a woman with strength, with power, with self-love and if that makes me a murderer then yeah. I am. Call me a murderer!

It's what you want, Fanuco?

FANUCO: It's not what I want, madam. I want you to live. Go peacefully. Go there so they can hear your story. Think of how many little girls and boys will grow up feeling that power that you feel if they knew you existed.

ASSATA: This is war, Fanuco. It's what we do to protect those we love. I love me and I love you. We have enemies coming for us, with death on their minds.

FANUCO: Then I will speak to them.

ASSATA: And say what?

FANUCO: Say that it was a mistake. That it's not really you.

ASSATA: Oh it's me alright. What's done is done.

Now what are you gonna do?

He's unsure what to do.

She watches him.

FANUCO: I don't know how to put it together.

She hands him the gun in her hand.

He holds it, shaking.

She then puts the pistol back together with the magazine.

ASSATA: There.

She hands him the weapon.

Point that at the door.

She goes to check the window.

What time are they getting here?

FANUCO: I don't know.

She gives him the phone.

ASSATA: Call them.

He dials.

(In Spanish.)

Hello, yes I am here. I have her. But I don't know how long I can hold her for. She's strong for an old woman. Okay, great.

Translation: Hola, sí, aquí estoy. La tengo aquí conmigo. Pero no sé si la puedo retener durante mucho más tiempo. Por cierto, menuda fuerza tiene para ser vieja! Ok, perfecto

He hangs up.

ASSATA: You didn't have to say the last bit.

FANUCO: But you are.

ASSATA: Don't ever be fooled and think that old age weakens you. In fact what I done seen and been through makes me stronger. So don't say I am strong for an old woman like it's news. Say it like it's a fact.

FANUCO: I'm sorry.

ASSATA: Don't be sorry.

> *She cocks the gun.*

Be ready.

Fanuco. Sing me that song your father used to sing to you.

FANUCO: Why?

ASSATA: If I go then I want to hear something sweet. Something African.

> *Knock knock!*

> *(Almost like a whisper.)*

Go open it.

> *He reluctantly goes to open.*

> *We watch him move in slow motion.*

Sing me the song, Fanuco.

> *FANUCO suddenly turns to face his teacher.*

FANUCO: I can't, madam.

> *He now points the gun at ASSATA.*

ASSATA: What are you doing?

FANUCO: There's things that I want for my family.

> *ASSATA with intent points her gun at FANUCO.*

ASSATA: You know I will do what I need to do to stay alive.

FANUCO: So will I.

An aggressive knock.

ASSATA: *That's* your enemy out there.

FANUCO: That's my family. *You're* the enemy.

ASSATA: Me? The woman that helped you find your voice?; the woman that saved your life? I showed you nothing but love, Fanuco! What have they done for you?

Another aggressive knock.

FANUCO: There are things I want so bad.

ASSATA: You won't get them this way.

FANUCO: But I can try. You're going to blame me for wanting to better life?

ASSATA: No, I can't blame you for that. But I worry that when you get those things it just won't be enough. It's not enough that you have a loving family and that you live in this beautiful country now you want to kill me so you can get more. What will my daughter have when I'm dead? I'm the only family she has.

FANUCO: I'm sorry.

ASSATA: There comes a time when you've gotta stop being sorry and start being brave and do what's right. Cuba has my heart, Fanuco. Take me out of here dead or alive and you will never have that freedom you need.

Never.

FANUCO: I don't believe in curses.

ASSATA: It's not a curse. It's a premonition. And I'm sure you know what that means.

Fanuco. Put down the gun.

Pause.

FANUCO: I can't, madam. I can't. Go peacefully, Assata. Just go peacefully.

> *She's conflicted.*

ASSATA: Fanuco, Fanuco.

> *A heavy pause before...*
>
> *The door is kicked in just as we snap to black.*
>
> *In blackout we hear...*

ASSATA: My brothers and sisters, my name is Assata Shakur and I am a Black Revolutionary.

I shouted but they didn't listen; I marched but they blocked my path; I cried but they remained unmoved.

So now I urge those who have grown tired of this corrupt system to join me in clenching their fists, banging on the walls to the oppressor's towers until they come crumbling down...Because only then will we take the power from the greedy and hand it to the people.

Power belongs to the people. So, go. Get yours!

> *End.*

WWW.OBERONBOOKS.COM

Follow us on www.twitter.com/@oberonbooks
& www.facebook.com/OberonBooksLondon

Printed in the USA
CPSIA information can be obtained
at www.ICGtesting.com
LVHW020940171024
794056LV00003B/879

9 781786 821096